Feminism

By

Alexandr Master

&

Tati Orly

Table of contents:

1. Beginning

From birth, no matter who we are, we are all equal. Boys and girls. There is no significant difference between us. We all start crawling, then walking, talking. All our development occurs at first in the same way. Later, we split up and prefer different games. Boys play with boys. Girls play with girls. When we are six or seven, we go to school and we are not all the same here.

Have you noticed that most boys do poorly in school, while girls do better in school? They are more diligent, more compliant. Boys only need to run, jump and fight. They can't sit still. Girls get much better grades in almost any subject, unlike their male peers. Physical development in boys at this point also begins to lag behind. As a rule, girls under the age of fifteen are always higher than boys. Despite this, boys are more athletic, and girls are more intellectually developed. There are exceptions, but mostly so. Girls get good certificates, and boys get sports scholarships.

After a while, the girls are no longer as diligent students. There is love, they want to walk and spend time with the boy. Grades are getting worse every day.

What do boys do in their place in such a situation? No, they won't sacrifice their studies for a girl. They will never put even one step of their beloved and, for example, preparation for a seminar. A boy will always choose to study. The girl, in general, will make a choice in favor of her boyfriend. Only those who have not met a guy, but have coped with their hormones, become excellent students. Or they didn't attach too much importance to it.

However, let's say that a girl achieves athletic results or plays the piano so that she becomes a prize-winner of competitions. You can imagine any other field where a girl can achieve good results. The simplest thing is that she gets a diploma with honors, and with it a great job offer, where you can not only earn good money, but also make an enviable career. A woman gets the opportunity to develop and be realized. Everything works out in the best way. She realizes her ambitions, dreams, goals.

All of a sudden, at one point, everything stops. A woman quits her job, gets married, and stands at the stove to cook. Maybe she's having a baby. Now the husband makes a career, and she becomes his shadow. They were choosing between her career and his, and the choice fell on his career. Why does a lottery like this make it necessary to choose husband's career? Why does a woman give in?

Giving in to her husband and helping him? Becomes a loyal assistant. Everyone can remember examples of such pairs. Everyone knows that behind any successful man, there is his wife who helps him.

A woman can endure a lot, can sacrifice a lot. Sometimes such a sacrifice is rewarded, and sometimes it is not. Not every husband is grateful to his wife for sacrificing her career, her success. Not everyone knows how to be grateful. There are situations when a woman remains abandoned by her husband. She doesn't have the career that she sacrificed, or the person for whom she made this sacrifice.

And she has to start all over again from the beginning. But she can't bring back the years. No perseverance. No sense of purpose. And most importantly, there is no confidence in her goals, which were in her youth. Only patience and calmness remained. There are still children to take care of and to make new sacrifices for. So passes the entire life of a woman who plays the role of a victim. First she sacrifices for her husband, then for the sake of the children. But this is not the end of her sacrifices. Children have grandchildren, and again a sacrifice is needed.

She went from being a successful woman to a patient housewife in just a few years. Now she has no ambitions of her own.

2. Woman and literature

Most of the literature is written by men. Do you know many recognized women writers? You can count them on your fingers. Although in reality, they are not so few. Women who write, a sufficient number. But they are not widely read, but they are criticized a lot. They cause a reaction. Let the poor, but the reaction. This is also a result. It is believed that women are only capable of writing women's primitive novels and detective stories.

Only here's the most amazing thing. After all, the bulk of readers are women. They are the ones who read male writers and don't read women. They criticize them. Then they are criticized by men. They face a barrage of criticism. Women themselves do not allow other women to be realized in the field of writing.

Men don't care, they read fiction with a few exceptions. In addition, writing does not bring the amount of money that men are used to, so they are not interested in this type of income.

Some smart women, in order to make their way in the field of writing, take a pseudonym and pass themselves off as a man. Very often, thanks to this, success is achieved. By the time the truth is revealed, readers are already completely in love with a writer with a male pseudonym.

For example, the writer George Sand. Under this pseudonym, the French writer Amandine Aurora Lucille Dupin was hiding.

The French writer wrote serious literature about independent and strong women. It is not known whether she would have been recognized if she had created under her real name. It is doubtful, especially since she wrote in the nineteenth century, when women were treated with prejudice and had virtually no rights.

The story of the creator of Harry Potter is very interesting: from a housewife, she turned into a billionaire woman. The writer's agent advised her to take a male pseudonym so that her books would be better bought. Again, we are talking about a disparaging attitude towards women writers.

And finally, the Russian author Max Fry. Initially, this pseudonym was used to hide a married couple who worked together, but later it turned out that most of the book was written by a woman. Now the woman hiding under this pseudonym Svetlana Martynchik writes without co-authorship, but under the same pseudonym.

Of course, these are not all examples available in the literature. These examples show what success can be if a woman takes a male alias.

The school curriculum for literature in some countries, and in particular in Russia, includes only reading by male authors. Women were given a place in poetry. Small, but stable.

Only somehow, there were women of a certain nationality and only one. There is no place for Nazism here, there is only place for one question: "why can women of only one nation - Jews, be the privilege of being poetesses?"

The University program also left place for women poetess. One of them is Sappho. She wrote a truly wonderful poem. A poetess who promotes the same-sex love of women for women. Why the curriculum gives us a strange example. She "seems to say" that if a woman is talented, if she can write poetry and leave a legacy behind her, then she is definitely a lesbian. Why are there so few heterosexual women in the literature? Where did they go? Can poems be written only by sexual minorities? Or are heterosexual women mediocre and stupid? It turns out so. Or the second option - why are there so few heterosexual women in literature? They are not allowed there. They have to take a male pseudonym in order to earn recognition.

3. Woman and the USSR

In pre-revolutionary Russia, women had an unenviable position. I am not talking about nobles or titled persons, we are talking about simple peasants. Such women were completely disenfranchised. They were treated like cattle and could even be killed. Anyone who is familiar with the work of the writer Dmitry Mamin – Sibiryak understands my words. It was Mamin-Sibiryak who described in detail in his works the hard life of an ordinary Russian woman.

A simple woman was very lucky if her master started inviting her to his house. Thus, she chose the role of concubine rather than the disenfranchised wife of a serf like her. Although it is not a question of choice, the Russian woman had no right to choose. Some caught their luck and became mistresses.

Sometimes they gave birth to their master and then became unnecessary as brides for Russian men. The peasant woman rejoiced at this outcome of things. She didn't want to be beaten by her husband, or killed for the slightest offense. There are so many examples in history of ordinary women being bullied.

The peasant women did not receive an education, even a primary education, before the Soviet Power came to Russia. Only after 1917 they were given the right to receive education. It was a very strong breakthrough. Thus, women did not get the opportunity to learn, but the opportunity to speak out and be free.

Besides the fact that women in the country received rights, the country itself received a completely new society. Lenin issued a decree not only "on land" and "on peace", but also "on the abolition of marriage" and "on the abolition of punishment for homosexuality".

Thus, the Soviet man was completely free from prejudices and moral restrictions.

At the end of 1918, a lesbian March was organized in Petrograd. In Moscow, there was a demonstration in which people walked completely naked, decorated with only red ribbons over their shoulders. The ribbons read: "Down with shame!".

The proletariat did not need clothes. It covers the beauty of the body. Waves of naked demonstrations were recorded across the country. So-called "Educational" processions were seen in Krasnodar, Sevastopol and other cities.

Every demonstration has an idea. The idea of a naked demonstration was not spared. The tradition of wearing clothes is a bourgeois relic. The proletariat doesn't need clothes. They are liberated and free. They don't need clothes to cover their bodies. If this motivation did not work, arguments were made for the idea of Darwinism.

A person was compared to an animal that didn't exactly need clothes.

By 1924, the demonstrations had become serious. The people were called out of a humiliating sense of shame. Contemporaries comment negatively on such demonstrations. They actively protested, but this did not affect the naked demonstrators. Women were freed from oppression, they were given rights, but they were not taught how to use them. At that time, women were illiterate and uneducated. They could not resist the sexual revolution, which not only allowed them to copulate with everyone they met, but imposed this so-called freedom on them.

According to the provisions of the Youth Union, which supported the right of free morals and included in its Charter a paragraph on sexual relations, every Komsomol girl was obliged to give herself to a Komsomol member at the first request, otherwise she was accused of philistinism. This clause of the Charter has existed for more than ten years.

With the same success, the theory of a glass of water was gaining popularity among young people. It was based on a complete denial of spiritual love, only on instincts. Sexual intercourse was supposed to be as simple as quenching your thirst with a single glass of water. Komsomol committees not only encouraged free relations, but also supported it in every possible way, organizing regular parties for young people to meet. At the end of such a party, the guys were asked to choose a girl who was obliged to enter into sexual contact with him, otherwise she could be excluded from the Komsomol.

Thus, a woman received the right to education, to work, and many other rights, but also received a sexual obligation, or more simply, fell into sexual slavery. Although in 1917, it was about women's equality, that is, about feminism.

But why did feminism turn into sexual violence? Was it equal if she couldn't refuse? Under the guise of feminism, women were raped. They just lied about women having rights.

The sexual revolution ended when Stalin came to power. I'm sure the women were very happy that they stopped being raped. Excessive looseness of morals is over. Sexual relations between men were again severely punished, and abortion was strictly prohibited. The family could only exist in monogamy. Premarital relationships, divorces, and infidelities were condemned. The political party concealed all material concerning the sexual revolution. About it could only tell the eyewitnesses of those events.

4. Woman and advertising

Over time, the Soviet Union's attitude to women has changed slightly. With the advent of the market economy, many products appeared on the market, which means that advertising was required in order to sell this product. Sellers often began to invite girls to work to advertise their product. Women are invited, as a rule, the appearance of the model.

Very often, not the women themselves are involved, but their body parts. Advertising exploits women's body parts to sell a product. A woman does not want to be exploited as a body or body parts, but at the same time she uses her charms and earns money from them. No one forces her to appear in such ads. No one forces her to take off her clothes. She does it herself. Does it for a fee. Women can choose, but do not enjoy this privilege.

Advertising images was a lot of fun the viewer. Everyone knows that the main goal of advertising is sales, and the more sales, the better. However, it is very common for so-called selling ads to exploit a woman or her body parts. Advertisers will do anything to make the customer happy. They do not disdain even outright clumsy work and unprofessionalism. Here are a few examples of popular ads that once got our eyes wet.

An advertisement for an insurance company (without names in this case) is shown on a poster of a woman of Korean appearance, next to which the inscription reads: "Bought a Korean woman? Get her fully insured." Of course, sex sells better than anything else in the world. Here, two egregious violations of human rights are immediately visible: Nazism and sexism. So, I want to answer: "insure yourself!".

Beautiful girls with big breasts from all sides offer loans, houses, cars. I remember the advertising slogan " do you want men to like you? Take out a loan to buy the car?". The consumer will definitely pay attention to such mediocre advertising. Maybe it will cause an unpleasant reaction, but what difference does it make? The main thing is that there is a reaction. This is what advertisers want.

What is surprising is that no one thinks about the fact that every ad has pros and cons. Not everyone will want the product of a company that ignores women's rights and uses them as sex slaves.

I still remember the mobile operator ad when it first appeared. The ad had overtly sexual content, but was very much remembered for centuries. An advertising poster showed a man lying on top of a woman, which read: "The connection is different – our safest." Despite the fact that advertising has long settled in the memory of unwitting viewers who had to see it on street billboards, this mobile operator does not exist for a long time. You can talk about cellular communications without mentioning sex. There is advertising in the world without sex, and without infringement of human rights. It's just that this kind of advertising is professional when it doesn't get personal.

Ads for well-known deodorants recently compared sweating women to pigs. And an ad for facial and body waxing products for women, which ran with the slogan: "Don't risk looking like a man!". This ad caused a wave of indignation around the world. How much can you tolerate outright ignorance?

Looking at modern advertising, it seems that the main interests of women are washing powder and mayonnaise. If you believe the ads, a woman should not go beyond women's Hobbies. Her Hobbies are as follows: washing, cooking, cleaning. There are women who do not "want anything, or even think" at all. "A woman should not think" – so says modern advertising. The manufacturer decides what is best for the woman, and she just consumes and nothing more.

With this kind of advertising, it's not about equal rights – there is no question of any rights at all. Women begin to believe that their humiliation is normal.

This Chapter was mainly about advertising in Russia. I do not want to say that this is the situation in all countries. This is still a small fraction of reality. Unfortunately, almost all Russian advertising is aimed at destroying women.

5. Women and the global sex slavery industry

Despite the fact that this is the twenty-first century and slavery has long disappeared, some countries have forgotten about it.

So, Thailand today has its main purpose - it is human trafficking. Village boys and girls are brought either to the cities of Thailand or to other countries of the world and forced into prostitution.

The current situation is that women, men and children are trafficked to other countries. Young girls are very often sold to European countries for rich old men. Most girls aren't even 18. At a very early age, they become sex slaves.

Often in Thailand, mothers themselves sell their daughters to pay off debts or survive in a difficult economic situation. This is not a disgrace or a reproach. Parents are often proud of their daughters who help them survive, even if they sell their bodies. It's lucky if the girl is married. No one at home will reproach her and accuse her of prostitution. For local residents - this is normal. They are so educated and women in particular. This is how their mothers raised them, and this is how they will raise their daughters. The culture is such that there is nothing wrong with selling your own child. Poverty in these countries is so extreme that people are not thinking about how to live, but only about how to survive in misery.

The second country where mothers themselves sell their daughters is Morocco. In the capital, Marrakech, you can buy a child of any age. There would be money. You can even buy a baby. This is a complete horror that occurs in modern society. So, in Europe or

Russia, a woman buys a designer bag, and in Marrakech you can buy a child. A child is not necessarily bought for good purposes – for adoption, for example. As a rule, children are bought, and girls in particular, for terrible and inhumane purposes. Unfortunately, the situation in the world is much more terrible than we imagine, it's just not accepted to talk about it. What they do with these children is anyone's guess. Mothers bring their own children to the market, not fruits and vegetables.

Sexual slavery became very popular in the 90s. A large number of women in Russia were left without work after the collapse of the Soviet Union and left for Europe and America in search of a better life. It is no secret that many of them became sex slaves, although they initially went to work as nannies and governesses.

The difficult economic situation in countries very often leads to the emergence of crime, and sexual slavery is the most frequent conductor of human poverty. In times of lack of funds, people are often gullible and fall into the hands of slaveholders.

Women are always the first in the risk group, as they always have someone to take care of, and therefore need to hurry to earn.

Western Europe has also suffered. Romania remembers how its borders were left by girls who went to work in dance cabarets, and ended up in brothels. Many of the girls never returned.

There are African tribes where women in infancy undergo surgery to remove the head of the clitoris. A large percentage of young girls die after this operation. Women all over the world have repeatedly raised the topic of sexual slavery; they are being listened to and measures are being taken. Some time passes and everything repeats again.

Sexual slavery is not always prostitution, it is also forced shooting in pornographic films. Women appear in pornography very often without their own consent. They are drugged to become weak-willed meat and take part in the shooting.

With the advent of the Internet, interest in this kind of film has subsided, and shooting has not become so profitable for the owners of film studios. Now there are a lot of home videos with explicit scenes on the Internet. Because of this, sexual slavery in the pornographic industry is not as relevant today as it was a few decades ago.

The development of prostitution also does not stand still. In most civilized countries, women are no longer kidnapped or forced into prostitution. A woman makes her own choice and becomes a prostitute at will. But it is still a respected profession in some countries. Men marry such women and have children with them, knowing their past. No one is more ashamed of this profession.

The growth of prostitution depends on the economic factor. The lower the level of the economy in a country, the higher the percentage of women who become prostitutes. And they earn in this way in economically developed countries. It is not surprising that young girls from Russia go to the Arab Emirates and Saudi Arabia to engage in prostitution. In this way, they improve the financial situation of their families. The same influx of girls of easy virtue is happening in England. It is for the reasons of a strong economy. Only in countries with strong economies there is a demand for prostitution, namely there are people who can pay for the services of such women.

6. Woman and sexual guides

Every now and then, on the Internet, you can come across calls about what a woman needs to do in order to keep a man. So-called experts give advice on how to behave if the relationship has cooled. The advice is mainly about the sexual part of the relationship. Unfortunately, this is not about family. About its creation and its development. It is not about the husband, but "about the boyfriend" and how to keep him. A woman who is busy with family development is unlikely to read this kind of article, but a girl can. And then the sexual guides come to the rescue.

A genre of literature that developed in ancient times, but reaches its peak of popularity at the present time. Such guides teach women to give a man pleasure in all possible ways. The emphasis is placed on the fact that a woman must be able to do a "deep Blowjob" or engage in anal sex in order to keep a man.

There are whole schools and courses on this subject. People earn a huge amount of money from single women who want to attract a man with their ability to do Blowjob. There are a lot of teachers of this skill and women of the ancient profession. And again, you can face the fact that prostitution is a respected profession, if they are not only authors of books, but also sex gurus. Women who do not engage in prostitution are so worthless that they need to be taught to have sex. With such women, a man does not want to be, since he needs to be restrained by a Blowjob or something else.

There is a substitution of moral values in society. It is imposed on a woman that she must be a prostitute, or at least behave as such, so as not to be left alone. A man admires a "skilled mistress" and throws an inept one. A woman is forced to behave in a way she doesn't want to. She is forced to be interested in sex, although she may be more interested in philosophy.

Sexual guides do not teach a woman to start a family. Now in general, such guides are not as popular as teaching Blowjob or anal sex. Women read such articles, reviews, posts or books with great interest, because it is now fashionable. This is now being promoted.

A huge number of trainings and courses called "deep throat". Women of all ages attend these courses. The main advertisement for such courses is a story that goes from mouth to mouth. The story is as follows: "a woman aged thirty-five plus Came to the course, learned to do deep Blowjob and immediately got married." And it works. Propaganda that only the ability to work your mouth properly will allow you to get married, even if you are about forty years old. No other abilities needed. Why are they, if a woman knows how to do a deep blowjob. Yes, even if it has some advantages - in the modern world this is not important. It is important to have only one skill and life will turn out the way society needs.

Everything became easier. Just a hundred years ago, women were fighting for the right to vote, and now they are fighting for the right to find a man. As if nothing else should interest her, except to satisfy a man and keep him for further satisfaction.

A man in this situation is also viewed in an unpleasant way. He was not interested in neither the appearance nor the character or mental quality. He is interested in a woman only the ability to make a Blowjob. Selfishness has spread to the intimate life. A man no longer wants to make an effort to please his woman. The world dictates that a woman must satisfy her man, otherwise he will leave her for another. Will go to the one who can do a deep Blowjob and with which there are no restrictions.

How many times has a woman had to hear that having sex with her is to have restrictions? This leads to the fact that she feels inferior and develops complexes in her. Is it right to force a woman to do what she doesn't want?

In a civilized society, sexual slavery is very professionally disguised. Now it's not as open as it used to be, but the point remains the same — to force a woman to do something she doesn't want to do.

7. Woman and public opinion

Every woman has faced the situation when her relatives or friends asked: "are You still alone? Do you have a boyfriend? Are you going to get married?" At the same time, such questions, for unknown reasons, are asked with compassion. The questioner seems to be crying, so much does it sympathize with the" lonely " woman. Paradoxically, the bulk of those interested are also women. Men are not interested in the personal life of their relative. They rarely ask such questions.

This question also needs to be answered correctly, otherwise you can face the disapproval or contempt of society. Why is it considered that a woman is afraid of loneliness? Why is it considered that a woman is devoid of any interests other than how to find a boyfriend or husband? In other words, all interests should be confined to the household.

Some people find it strange if a woman chooses a different type of activity than a household. It frankly does not understand and does not accept society, or rather other women. The male half of society, I repeat, is completely indifferent to what a woman does and why she is alone or not alone.

Suddenly it happens that a woman does not marry, but gives birth. It happened, it happens. Gave birth to children, but still alone. And she faces such neglect. Every woman is sure to tell her at a convenient time what she brought in the hem.

It starts with the maternity home. The nurse is sure to smile when it comes to the fact that the mother does not visit the father of the child.

When the child grows up and it is time to go to school, not all schools will be ready to accept a child from a single-parent family. This practice exists in Russia at the moment. This is unofficial, but the headmaster of a good school will always ask about the state of the family and say that they prefer children who have a father and mother. At first, a woman is judged for her choice not to marry, and then her child.

A woman should not stand out and be individual. It should not go beyond the accepted norms. Every woman has such a program: school, Institute, marriage, mortgage, children. And you can't leave it. If you move away, be silent. The whole country goes shopping with her husband on Saturdays, and you are against it – keep quiet. Don't you dare stand out. A woman does not go shopping with her husband on Saturdays for one reason – she does not have a husband.

There is no one to go with, and therefore does not go. There is no other reason.

There are many women in the world who can't have children. This is not because she doesn't want to, although it also happens. Not all women want to become mothers – and this is also normal. She doesn't want to and it's her choice. But there are women who want a child but can't give birth. They undergo numerous courses of treatment in order to get pregnant, but they still do not succeed. Such a woman is psychologically very vulnerable. And no, to show sympathy, people around her once again humiliate her by asking constant questions: "Not pregnant?", "not going to give birth?". These questions are again asked by women. Why are our women so stupid as to ask such questions? Do they not understand that this is, at least, rude. Where is the tact and good manners of women? Why are they so cruel? Where is their female solidarity?

In men, there is male solidarity. Even if men frankly can't stand each other, the question of male solidarity does not even need to be raised.

Women, on the contrary, they will never support a woman. Not even if this woman is a close person. She would never support a woman like that. Maybe that's why they say that female friendship doesn't exist. They don't know how to be friends. They have no compassion, no empathy. If another woman feels bad – this is a reason to be happy, not a reason to provide support.

There are exceptions in any sphere of relations. Happiness, when women, no matter what, know how to be kind and loving. This is real luck.

8. Woman and cosmetology

One day I heard the following revelation from a friend: "There's no point in you meeting someone. You are old and you will be alone."

I was thirty-four years old at the time. And we talked about where you can meet men with women and Vice versa. Thanks to this remarkable truth, I understood the answer to a burning question. Why is cosmetology popular? Women are literally mad in the pursuit of youth. Every self-respecting woman always did something with the face, not counting the basic care. Beauty shots are all for young people. For more adult ladies – adult procedures, in the form of fillers and Botox injections. Grown-up ladies are as old as I am at thirty-four.

A young girl comes to a cosmetologist at the age of eighteen. Comes to clean the face. Wanting a face with clean skin is a perfectly normal desire for a young girl. Almost every cosmetologist begins to give lectures about the prevention of cosmetic procedures. Young, and even rather small girls, are advised at such an early age to inject beauty injections for adult women.

The multi-million dollars cosmetology industry created by men is not aimed at maintaining beauty, but primarily at pumping out money.

To maintain beauty, you do not need a lot of procedures and expensive ones, too. It is enough to visit the cosmetologist's office periodically. But the industry wants more. It wants every woman, regardless of age, to depend on cosmetology.

From each tube, women are told that men will not like it if they do not pump a liter of silicone into their lips and turn them into disgusting dumplings. A woman obediently performs what is imposed on her. Although, if you ask the men: "what do they think about the silicone in the lips?". Almost every sane man will answer that he does not like such lips. He loves naturalness. He doesn't like overly made-up women. Almost all men will answer in a voice that they are for naturalness, not artificiality.

The same goes for the chest. Some idiot made a comment to a woman about her small Breasts, and all she does is run to a plastic surgeon with a desire to get her Breasts done. For the most part, artificial Breasts look ridiculous. The nipples look in different directions. When a woman is lying down, her chest does not fall, but stands erect. This is very funny. You should never pay attention to comments about appearance. After all, such remarks are made by ill-mannered people. A person with a good upbringing will never allow himself to make someone a comment about appearance, and even more about breast size. This is the same as telling a man a comment about the size of his penis. A normal woman wouldn't do that.

Currently, the most popular plastic surgery in Russia is narrowing the vagina. Yes, women are seriously concerned about the size of their vagina. This is written in social networks. Women consult each other about this. They get the impression that a man will not want them if suddenly her vagina becomes a little wider. Hence, cesarean section instead of natural birth became very popular. A woman is ready to cut her belly several times with the words: "I want to be wanted." They really believe that the vagina becomes the size of a bucket after giving birth.

You can't change their minds. The Russian woman is very concerned that she will become unnecessary to a man, without whom she very often has no sense to live. Unfortunately, this is media propaganda. If a man wants to break up – no narrow vagina can hold him.

It is not always the decision to make a similar operation to narrow the vagina or give birth by cesarean without medical indications – this is the initiative of a woman, sometimes her man insists on it. A man insists on what he has no right to insist on. This is akin to rape. Dictate what to do with the body.

In Russia, where there are far fewer men than women, women fight for the right to be with a man in any way, sometimes even the most sophisticated. They are afraid to grow old, because there are sad statistics that say that the old wife is changed to a younger one. Women are afraid to stay on the sidelines and go for help to cosmetology and plastic surgery.

9. Woman and men's infidelity

Continuing the topic of the ratio of the number of men and women, we will touch on the topic of male infidelity.

Many women forgive infidelity because of the fear of loneliness. This is because women believe that there are far fewer men than women. We are talking about Russia. Although according to statistics, boys are born much more than girls and up to 39 years of men more than women. That is, just at the age when families are created. There are exceptions, of course, but still – this is a rarity than a pattern.

In principle, if a woman wants to, she can create a family without any problems. There are enough men for everyone. The second issue is that there is a very high percentage of men who are addicted to drugs and alcohol. A woman wants a better man for herself and therefore often agrees to the role of a mistress, but a man who is not dependent on alcohol and drugs. She becomes the mistress of a man who already has a family – a married man. No one criticizes such women. Such women are pitied.

The Siberian and Ural regions are particularly popular for so-called polygamy. Of course, this is not polygamy in the literal sense of the word, as, for example, in some Muslim countries.

We are talking about the fact that men in Siberia and the Urals often have a second family. The first and official family does not know about the existence of the second. The second woman knows that she is in a relationship with a married man. And the most interesting thing is that there is nothing wrong with it. No one judges such women. No one judges such men.

A conviction will only occur if a man chooses one woman out of two. If he continues to live on two families - normal. Some people live like this all their lives. The wife may never know that the husband has a mistress. And that's half the trouble. Most likely, the mistress gave birth to a child. Maybe more than one. Brothers and sisters don't know about each other.

This was acceptable in Russia after the second world war, but there was a different situation. There are no men left. Many women have allowed their man to cheat for a single purpose. A man cheated on a woman and at the same time helped another. Another woman got pregnant, raising the country's demographics. In the post-war period, no one can say anything bad about such men. They are still heroes, just as they were during the war.

Currently, a man behaves the same way, because a woman is used to giving indulgences to a man who is a traitor. If he stays with two at once, it is bad, but tolerable. But if he decides to leave one family – he's a scoundrel.

Constant propaganda in the cinema that a man can cheat on a woman. Family values have lost value. American cinema does not carry such information. I haven't seen treason propaganda there for a long time. Russian cinema touches on treason in almost every film. Men's infidelity.

Almost all Russian cinema teaches women to suffer, to feel sorry for. It doesn't teach a woman to respect herself. It doesn't teach to love. She must be weak-willed and therefore forgive everything, including treason. In the end, society will condemn her if she doesn't forgive. No one should stand out. Why do other women forgive and continue to tolerate the traitor, and she decided to remember her pride? No, all women and everyone should live the same way-suffer. A woman must suffer and sacrifice herself. Otherwise, what kind of Russian woman is this? Suffer and endure.

10. Woman and her role in society

For centuries, the role of women has been reduced to the birth of children and the preservation of the home. A man also has similar roles. He becomes a father and breadwinner. These are natural functions. Nature gave them to us. There is nothing wrong with them. Now a lot of people say that a woman does not have to. And you know they're right.

A woman doesn't have to. Just like a man, he doesn't have to. There is even a whole direction called "child free". A woman may not give birth to children, a woman may not be a housewife. But the truth is that in Russia it has no special opportunities to be realized in any other field.

America has gone far in terms of women's freedom and equality. An American woman marries late or never. She gives birth when she wants to. The benefit is the ability to freeze their eggs. An American woman doesn't need a man to start a family, she needs him for sex. Despite the fact that such a woman is attractive, she does not use it. She doesn't sell herself or her body. This does not apply to Russia.

A Russian woman can't make a career if a man doesn't help her. Only a man can help her in life. You can't do without it. Lucky for those girls who are born in the family of a domineering father. Lucky for those women who will marry a powerful man and then, if he wants, he will help in his career.

A Russian woman is often forced to enter into sexual relationships for the sake of a career. If an American woman engages in sexual relations for the sake of a career – this is a scandal and equates to harassment. Russian women enter into such relationships because-this is the norm. Otherwise, you will spend your entire life working at a mediocre job and getting mere crumbs for your work.

Men in Russia will never let a woman into a high-paying job. She is worthy of this job, if she is his wife. At the moment, the highest paid job is the civil service. But not at the bottom, but, for example, in the legislative authorities. Do you see many women there?

They are practically non-existent. They put a few in plain sight, so that no one would think that women are being harassed in Russia. And in fact, how many women there are as a percentage of men. One percent? The majority of enterprises, of course, belong to men. Women are simply not allowed in there. There are a lot of jokes about this in Russia. Women are often compared to a chicken or a sheep. A priori, a woman can't be smart. It's inherently stupid. And if a woman is stupid, her job is to serve a man.

In conclusion, I want to say about the woman driving. Everyone knows, and even men, that a woman is a more accurate driver. Although jokes about the fact that "a woman driving is a monkey with a grenade" are omitted not only by men, but also by women. Women also poison each other. No woman will ever support another.

Perhaps this is the reason why a woman is forced to ask for support from a man. And he will do as he sees fit. Will support it at its discretion. And this is bound to happen through sexual relationships. A man can't just help you. Always in return for sex. And this has been happening for years. For years, women have been forced to engage in sexual relations in exchange for respect. Although, this is a big illusion. It's only getting worse. No one respects, and even condemn.

Imagine, for example, a producer who married a young actress. The actress is talented, but who pays attention to it. Other women envy her and hate her. No one will say that she is talented. But the fact that she is married to a producer and is therefore being filmed. The Producer will not shoot a mediocre actress, even if it is his wife. A man always thinks about reputation. Let's say the film is a failure and it can't earn money, which means it won't get the budget for the next film either.

The paradox lies in the fact that the films look with pleasure, and immediately spread unpleasant gossip. To earn the trust of society, and above all, of women, it must take many years. The bill goes on for decades. There are a lot of such examples in Russian cinema. Of course, there are exceptions and not always the actress is talented. But for the most part, women who are talented are humiliated. No

one pays attention to the incompetent.
Nothing to be envious of.

11. Woman and obligations

First date and now a man invited you for coffee. How often does a woman pay for herself in this situation? How often does a woman pay for herself in Russia for dinner in a restaurant? In the majority of civilized countries, this question is not worth it at all. There, the couple goes to a restaurant for dinner and each pays for itself. A woman doesn't want to become dependent. She doesn't want to bear any liabilities to the fact that men paid for her coffee at a cost of three dollars. In many southern European countries, a man buys a woman coffee and sincerely believes that she is obliged to give him sex in return. To prevent such situations from occurring, a woman often either refuses refreshments or pays for herself. And why make the situation worse when you can avoid it?

In Russia, it is not customary for a woman to pay for dinner. Russian women, with rare exceptions, value their freedom. Rather, it seeks to become dependent. There is an opinion among women that "the more a man pays for you, the more he loves you." The woman not only does not pay the bill in the restaurant, but also tries to give her other bills to the man. She herself seeks complete dependence.

Here, a woman is not considered successful if she has made a career. It is considered successful with a rich man.

Mothers tell their daughters that they need a rich man. The mother does not tell her daughter that she needs to learn foreign languages, read books, study art. She advises only to find a rich man. From early childhood, she gives her daughter to sports so that she has a beautiful body that she will catch a man on.

Sex acts as a weapon. No need to care for a woman. She herself will jump into bed. She was so taught. Everywhere there is propaganda that a man can be attracted in two ways: sex or intelligence. The easiest way is sex. Sex is now the cheapest product, which is abundant in the market, but there is no demand. Men stopped giving sex as much importance as a few decades ago. There are more than enough women who are ready to have sex now. While in more developed countries, women do not hurry to have sex. The man, in turn, is also extremely careful, since he can be accused of sexual harassment.

In general, men in Russia should be happy that they are in a better position. Women have few rights and freedoms, so a man is almost always right. If a situation suddenly arises in

Russia that a woman accuses a man of sexual harassment. For example, at work. As a rule, the outcome in Russia is known. No one will support such a woman. She will become an outcast because it is her own fault. The women themselves are the first to blame her for this. There will be no solidarity. It was her own fault. She gave a reason. Behaves like a prostitute, so she was harassed. A man in this situation will always be a victim. The whole society, absolutely, will side with the man. There will only be exceptions if we are talking about a child. I will not touch on this topic. Adult Russian women who find themselves in a situation of violence are almost always silent. They rarely go for help. They will never get it. This happened because there were cases when a woman was not raped, but she stipulated. There were many such cases. They didn't beat the woman, but she slandered. But it is impossible to judge all women on several occasions.

The topic of violence against women is very acute and unpunished. She will hear: "it's her own fault", and therefore she is silent. Who wants to make themselves look like a whore? In principle, nothing has changed since pre-revolutionary Russia. Except that they don't kill women, and if they do, they serve time in prison. I have met women who were married and said that their husbands periodically raped them against their wishes. It's just not accepted to complain about it. In fact, the point is not what is accepted and what is not. The thing is that there is no support. A woman does not know where to go with her misfortune. Here, she will go to her mother, and she will say: "endure, rich husband." That would be the end of all her violence. Next time, she won't complain, but say that everything is fine. I had a friend who was systematically beaten by her husband. Once he knocked out her teeth. When her friends and acquaintances asked: "how are you doing?", my friend always smiled broadly and said: "we are doing well." She said this with tears in her eyes, but everyone believed her. No one knew that she was living in a nightmare. Only after the divorce, she told us that she was constantly raped and severely beaten. Her mother knew, but she didn't say anything. She was silent because it was not accepted. It is not customary to say that her daughter lives poorly. We all have "everything is fine".

Sometimes a cup of coffee can result in violence, not in coffee grounds.

12. Woman and the social movement

In itself, the movement in defense of women's rights - feminism, has not gained popularity in Russia. For some reason, women involved in prostitution spoke about protecting the rights of women.

They arranged meetings where they undressed and showed their naked Breasts. These women have spoiled feminism and created a bad impression of feminist women. Why in Russia and Ukraine can a feminist necessarily be a prostitute? They fight for equality, but in fact they sell their bodies and bare their Breasts. Equal rights do not mean going bare-chested in public places. Do men go naked? So why equal rights is necessarily something unpleasant. Few people are happy to look at a strange girl with bare Breasts. This is probably why the women's rights movement is not developed in Russia, because many people associate it with something naked and unpleasant.

Feminist literature is written in a decent amount, but again in Russia it has not received distribution. There are almost no Russian authors. Many authors of women are American. Unfortunately, the books of some active feminists have not yet been translated into Russian. They are printed only in the original language, that is, in English. Not everyone can read literature written in English. It is not clear why this was done. Maybe because there is no demand for such literature. Maybe from the fact that none of them showed any interest in such literature.

In any case, the strange thing is that the majority of women who actively fight for women's rights, that is, feminists – in real life, women are lesbians. They fought so hard for their rights that men became afraid of them?

Or did they fight so hard for equal rights with men that they took over their rights? This is my personal observation. I have nothing against non-traditional women. I'm just stating the facts.

I also want to note that in countries where feminism is particularly active, homosexuality is very developed. I'm for real feminism! For feminism that does not promote same-sex love. For a feminism where men are not afraid of women.

Why do we only have extremes? In Russia, where only men have power in all spheres of life: in everyday life, in politics, in business. The woman is forced to make concessions and completely submit to the man. In Russia, women have almost no rights. On paper, Yes. For example, she can vote and get a driver's license. This has nothing to do with reality. If a woman can't make a career without a man's help, then she has no rights. No rights from the word "completely".

In other countries, where rights are equal between men and women, but where men have become afraid of women. They have become so afraid of being accused of sexual harassment that it is easier for them to have a relationship with each other than with a woman.

This is again the subject of television, cinema, and mass media. How many similar stories. A man flirts with a woman, then invites her over. She agrees. They enter into an intimate relationship. The next day, he's a maniac, accused of sexual harassment. His career, family, and so on are collapsing. How will his life develop in the future? Why won't anyone take his side? Why is the victim here a woman? Wasn't a man hurt after sex? Didn't he lose his job and family?

Why these extremes? Where are the honest rights of women and men? Where there is real equality. In the end, men will become so afraid of women that they will stop having families at all. The result will be even more interesting if men start claiming their rights and being harassed. And in the near future it may well be so.

13. The prevention of violence

Rape statistics can't be real, because women are silenced. They keep silent about what happened to them completely consciously. As I said above, they are afraid of being "guilty". A woman is being abused and instead of receiving support and sympathy, she is being judged and left alone. She has nowhere to go in this terrible situation. The woman is left completely alone. Although, recently, centers for women who have been subjected to violence have been organized. The number of these centers and the number of women who need such centers are disproportionate.

A woman who provokes a rapist is usually not against it. We will not speak of such women. We will touch upon the topic of not just violence against women, but the prevention of violence. There will be much fewer victims if the crime prevention is properly developed.

Imagine a dating situation. A man meets a woman on the Internet, as is now common. An epistolary connection is formed between them. They exchange photos and personal data. They discuss hobbies, work, weather, and travel. They are satisfied with absolutely everything in each other. Sympathy turns into love. And now, finally, the long-awaited meeting. They drink tea and talk sweetly. He offers to accompany her. At some point their hands would touch and she would decide to invite him home. Of course, he agrees and then tea is not limited. Comes to the aid of heavier artillery: wine or champagne. The woman quickly gets drunk, and the man begins to undress her. She resists, but can't do anything but say something: "no, and not today." Everything happens fast enough and hurts for a woman. A man wants to have sex "without restrictions", as he says.

The woman did not plan to have sex at all. She was very honest when she asked to come in. The invitation was only for a glass of wine, and then a taxi. She hadn't planned for the invitation to turn into an intimate relationship.

The man left in the morning. She didn't hear or see him again, and she didn't want to. She was alone with her pain. It is quite possible that she will begin to blame herself for inviting and therefore - it is her own fault. It is for this reason that she will not tell anyone and will perceive this situation as a terrible shame. She won't tell anyone, not even a close friend. She will be afraid of being judged.

And life goes on. Continues with pain and frustration. How many years would it be before she told anyone? Maybe never.

There are many such situations. I am sure that every woman or her friend has it in stock. Sometimes women share these stories with each other.

Another similar case may occur with a woman at work. She got a job, but her career isn't moving. Suddenly a man from the management team, or maybe the boss himself, makes her signs of attention.

The woman didn't like him, but the man clearly gives to understand that in case of its failure is dismissal, and in the case of consent – promotion. This choice is very often faced by a woman. It's not easy to find a new job. A woman is sometimes forced to agree to enter into an intimate relationship with a boss, in order not to lose income for her family. This relationship can last as long as want, but the increase is unknown – to happen or not. Probably not. In such a situation, a woman cannot complain anywhere. She is not protected. Run to her senior management, who are also men? No one is going to listen to her, much less defend her. In civilized countries, women are protected from sexual harassment at work.

If suddenly there is a connection between colleagues at work, they are immediately called to the human resources department for a conversation. The HR specialist is interested in two questions. First: was there any coercion on the part of the man? Second: does he not make do what a woman does not want? Initially, the higher management sides with the woman. This is fine because a man will think twenty times before showing signs of attention to a woman. He wouldn't force her. He's scared. Because if a woman doesn't like it, she won't tolerate it.

She can stand up for her honor. To rape a woman and go unpunished in a civilized country is a big mistake. Every reasonable man understands this. This is the prevention of crime, and in particular – rape. The man understands that he will be punished and does not do anything for which he can be held responsible.

In third world countries, a man is not responsible. The time when a man took responsibility for an intimate relationship has long been forgotten. Now it's all the woman's fault. Not only men but women themselves shout about this guilt. They blame other women, forgetting that they are treated the same way. Women are never in solidarity. They have no empathy for other women.

14. Woman and solidarity

Here we come to the solidarity of women, which will be discussed in this Chapter. There is a stereotype that there is no female friendship. Perhaps this happened because there is no female solidarity. A woman basically will never support another woman. It does not matter whether it is an acquaintance or not, a friend or foe, a relative or a stranger.

You can be friends for several years, and even support each other in everything. But as soon as one of you gets married. This is the end of friendship, which means solidarity, too. A married woman will always side with her husband, even if he is wrong. She will give up friendship in a second, without thinking.

The same thing happens when an unmarried woman begins to put an ultimatum in choosing her or her husband. An unmarried woman always loses. If a similar situation occurs in men - here you do not need to go far for examples. A man, in most cases, will choose friendship. He won't even choose. A man always divides. Friendship for a man is friendship, and a woman for him is a woman.

There are men who will never make a choice between a woman and a job. A man can distinguish.

In a woman, everything is somehow miraculously intertwined. It connects work and home, friends and men. Because of what then suffers.

When a woman is faced with a choice – who to date: a married or a free man, the woman will not hesitate – the choice will be made in favor of a married man. There are several reasons for this. First, a married man is valuable because he is already ready for family life. You don't have to teach him anything. He knows how to handle a woman "at home". Secondly, a married man gives the impression that he is good and decent. If he is married, then he is needed, and if he is needed, then he is an enviable target. And finally, the third reason is very feminine. A woman wants to prove to another woman that she is better. She is not interested in other people's grief, other people's problems. A single man is rarely attractive.

A common situation when a single man begins to date a woman. And suddenly, out of nowhere, a thousand fans appear. Everyone immediately remembers him. Before that, they did not notice him. But as soon as he became "busy" - they immediately remembered him. Everyone abruptly needed him. He became necessary even for married women. They are ready to divorce, for his sake. Leave their husbands and children, just to be near such an enviable groom, until this time unnoticed.

Women's solidarity works in reverse and is intertwined with envy. A woman tells good things about her family life. God forbid. She immediately has detractors. A woman a priori cannot be happy with her husband and her life.

If a woman does not say bad things about her husband, then others will talk about him. Whether they know him or not is the tenth thing. They'll think of it and report it. A woman should be unhappy. Only in this case can we expect solidarity. Otherwise, it will not be there and there is nothing to hope for.

Women can't be happy for other women. Recently, I came across a discussion on the Internet about a movie based on a novel of the same name written by a woman. The main role of the film was also played by a woman. A well-known actress who combines social activities with her work. She helps many sick children.

How many angry reviews were heaped on the film. The same negative reviews were awarded to the actress and writer. Despite the fact that the book was a world bestseller and sold in twenty-four countries, and the actress is in demand. The book is written correctly. Threats were also made to the actress directly. She was cursed.

At the same time, several months before that, there was a film adaptation of a film based on a novel written by a man. The leading role was also played by a famous actor - a man. The film was rather weak. The book was a bestseller only in a single country. Reading the book was very difficult because of an illiterate presentation. The author brought a great idea to life, but revealed it in a clumsy way. Not a word of negativity about the film, not a word about the book, and not a word about the actor. Men. They are not spoken badly of.

They speak poorly of women. Men are spoken badly of only by their women and no one else. Public opinion applies only to women. As they just do not call. It gets to the point where a married woman is branded a lady of the demimonde. This is an insult that almost all women can afford to say about another.

Sometimes it seems that women hate absolutely everyone: men, women, children, and even themselves.

15. Woman and men's pleasures

Many women will agree with me when I say that the vast majority of men want three-way sex, where the third is another woman.

Many trainings on this subject, where the personal growth coach agitates: "If your woman is against threesomes, find another woman. Find someone who agrees."

Quite often, such experiments occur in couples who already have children and not one. A man offers a woman such an experiment with a subtext that otherwise he will get a mistress. And here everything is under the supervision of a permanent woman. You don't have to be afraid of anything. She can participate herself. I don't think women agree to this with pleasure. Very often they are forced to agree and make concessions to their man. They do not want to destroy the family and agree to participate in an orgy. And then, more. A man does not stop and is not satisfied with a threesome just once. Such experiments are firmly embedded in their sexual life and are fixed there as something familiar. Many women suffer such humiliation. Many begin to fight for their rights through alcohol. In any case, it doesn't end with anything good.

There are also more deplorable cases – when the woman refuses and then the man acts as he was advised by the personal growth coach. He really breaks up with his woman and goes in search of another, more compliant.

Another interesting direction is Swingers. There are websites and clubs where people who want to switch partners get together. On some sites, you can find such a partner if you don't already have one. Swinger clubs operate all over the world and have become widely popular. People work all week just to go to a Swinger club with their woman on Friday and watch another man have her while you have another woman.

The initiator of visiting such clubs in most cases is a man. A man who wants to cheat, but in a more sophisticated way. He also trusts and "values" his partner, so he prefers to enter into sexual relations with another woman at constant. In the eyes of the one that "loves". In this situation, what rights can a woman have at all? Her opinion doesn't count, much less her rights. Only a man has rights, and in particular to his woman, too. Wanted to put it under someone else's man. Wanted to, under another woman.

Fear of loneliness turns a woman into a weak-willed rag who is silent and does what she does not like. Every week, she has to go with her man to these clubs in order for him to stay with her.

Finally, the last thing I want to focus on in this chapter is sex life in general.

Quite often, a woman is going to make concessions to their partner in bed. And this is not fiction. Any woman will agree with me when I ask - how often does she give in to her man sexually? Does she always have consensual sex?

Was there never a time when she was forced? A man likes to have sex "without restrictions". At the same time, a woman experiences these restrictions on herself. She doesn't want to, but her opinion is again uninteresting. With extreme exceptions, a man will be interested in the desires of his woman.

The woman always gives in. All she does is give in, putting her own interests in the background. Eventually, forgetting your desires completely.

16. Substitution of moral values

"The family is always a bad thing. Being a wife is bad, but being a mistress is good. If you get married, make sure you get a lover.". This is the current propaganda in social networks. Married women who preach classic family values are laughed at. From all sides, they hear that the husband is a subhuman and he will definitely cheat. People do not have the concept of family from the word "completely". A huge number of children who grew up without a father - this is the result of the fact that the institution of the family does not exist. This happens from generation to generation.

A married woman always sees her husband in an unpleasant way. Sometimes he's fat and unshaven, sometimes he smells bad, sometimes he slurps. A married man is always a kind of "animal" in the house, who lies on the sofa, drinks beer and does nothing.

A single man is always different - handsome, smart, able-bodied, and most importantly, generous. Need to have a relationship with him. In any case, you cannot get married. This is all prejudice. The stamp in the passport is doing its dirty work. It turns a man into an unwashed animal.

A married man is also fine. Destroying someone else's family is normal. A married woman is always a source of evil and stupidity. A married woman can only be normal if she herself has a lover. A loyal and loving woman is bad.

All these substitutions of moral values come from social networks. Journalists write about this. They inculcate norms of behavior in society. Don't love - this is bad. Don't be faithful – it's not fashionable. You can do other things. You can have promiscuous sexual relations and not respect your husband. That's cool. If a woman loves and is loved – the anger of others will fall on her. Television is also not far behind. The wife is shown in many films always angry and dissatisfied, ugly and unkempt. While the mistress always looks cheerful and happy. Spending time with a mistress is so natural. Spending time with your family is unnatural.

Women are as if under hypnosis. The husband must be humiliated, destroyed, disrespected. He is a source of income for his wife and nothing else. Suddenly husband had a bad time. Let's say he was fired from his job or the business does not bring the usual income, as before. The woman should expel him for being unnecessary.

The man is no longer needed. He cannot be loved. He only has to and nothing else. Three skins must be removed from him, otherwise why is he still needed.

This is delivered in the form of instructions from mothers, mothers from grandmothers, and so on around the circle. Daughters will grow up and begin to teach their daughters in the same familiar way. And this is not surprising, because their mothers were not taught to respect their family. They were not taught to bear responsibility for the person with whom you connect your fate - for your husband. The husband "must" bring money. As long as he brings it, it's the husband. As soon as he stops bringing, you can drive him out of the house like a dog. Very convenient position.

Every woman hears constantly: "don't get married." It's like something terrible is happening. Although, everything should be simple here and it can't be simpler. If a woman wants to get married, let her. If she doesn't want to get married, let her.

A woman is constantly being dictated how to live her life. She can't decide for herself how to live. Why? All they do is teach her. First, parents who themselves do not know how? Then the teachers, who were also offended by fate. At a more mature age, she is taught by the media, television. Everyone is guided by the fact that a woman does not know how to make decisions on her own, implying that she is stupid. She can only execute commands.

Told her on social media: "get a lover." She gets a lover. It's time to fight back and not go along with the mass suggestion of the media, social networks, and television. Why does a journalist or blogger tell women how to live? Women have their own heads on their shoulders and only they decide how and what to do with their lives.

17. Consequences of a request for protection and justice

Nobody will ever blame the victims of the robbery for lying. Victims of sexual abuse are almost always. I am sure that every reader will agree that an adult woman rarely expects protection in the event of sexual harassment.

She goes to the police for help, but gets no help. She gets only sidelong glances and reproaches that she should not go in such provocative clothes and not give a reason. She is told that it is her own fault. She was abused through her own fault. A woman begins to fight for her safety, and what does she get in return? She gets a tongue-lashing. "Stay at home and keep your head down. Maybe then you won't be raped."

The most paradoxical thing is that it does not depend on how old she is. Very often you can hear such reproaches and addressed to children. That is, girls who have been abused are often to blame themselves, too. Little girls give an excuse to be raped while sitting in a sandpit in a short dress. And such reproaches are thrown not so much by men as by women themselves.

Here is an interesting example. In a provincial city, several sexual maniacs were brutalized. They in number of three people tracked down the victim, as a rule at the railway station, which only came to the big city from the village. The girls were all about eighteen or twenty. Naive rural girls.

Two of them approached her and offered to take her where she needs. Of course, not for free, but as a taxi. The girl did not see anything wrong with being taken to her destination by taxi. It's late, and here men are so responsive.

Everything is not terrible alone in an unfamiliar city. The two men were taking her to the forest, where a third was waiting. All three of them took turns raping the victim and then brutally killing her. There were several dozen such crimes by the time their identity was established. The criminals were arrested, judged, and jailed. It seems justice has been served, but the girls ' lives can't be returned. But here's what's interesting about this situation. One of the criminals was married. The wife fully supported her husband not only during the criminal process, but also after. She waited for him like the most loyal woman. She said that all the victims are to blame and now she is forced to stay without her husband. So, the victims are to blame for being raped by three men and then brutally killed. They are to blame for their own death. As the years passed, the criminals got out of prison. The most interesting thing is that this woman's husband left her. The reason was that she supported him. Yes, he had told her that she was neither a woman nor a human being to justify such a criminal, even if it was her husband. And he's right.

What is the matter with a woman who could justify such atrocities? And how many women in our society who are waiting for such rapists or murderers from prisons? How many women who connect their fates with rapists and give birth to children from them? I personally know a few of these women.

Often a woman is left alone with her grief. She turns to the police for help, where she is accused of lying. She seeks help from her mother, who does not believe her and believes that her daughter is inventing. There is no talk of acquaintances who will not even believe it.

Why go and tell your pain if no one will believe you? There are not enough centers where victims of violence are supported. There are not enough funds to hire good psychologists to work in these centers. In our society, we are used to the fact that all help is given to us for free, but this is wrong. And the aid that we pay taxes on is not provided to us. No one is outraged. No one will say: "why don't you protect me if your salary is made up of my taxes?"

Law enforcement agencies are not obligated, but volunteers are. Criminals know that they will almost certainly go unpunished, which means that crimes will be committed again and again. We are not talking about a humane society. There is no place for violence against women in a humane society.

18. Domestic violence

The husband beats the wife. Beats regularly and brutally.

The topic of domestic violence is so relevant that no matter how much they talk about it, the situation does not get better.

The situation does not get better, because there is no punishment and no fear that there will be a reckoning for what has been done. The absence of consequences frees hands as much as possible in the physical sense. That is, how much physical strength a man has, so much he can use force against the women of his family. This is not only about violence against the wife, but also against the daughters. Almost always, a man who beats his wife will also beat his daughter.

It is absolutely impossible to resist a man who beats a woman. The woman is constantly scared. Her whole life is spent in fear and fear for her own life. She is afraid to sleep, afraid to eat, afraid to be alone with her husband, afraid to talk. But the worst thing here is different. Such women are afraid to ask for help.

A woman will ask for help, and in return she will be attacked again: "it's her own fault", "where did you look before", "leave your husband". That is, in return, she will not get help, but only useless advice. First, men who beat their wives, as a rule, before marriage were just sweethearts and bunnies. Secondly, sometimes there is nowhere to go. For example, a woman came out of the house with a child, or maybe with two, and where should she go? Right or left? Then what? Go to a center for women who have been victims of domestic violence. But such centers may not be in her small city.

Can you imagine what anger will fall upon her if her husband finds her? In most cases, a woman is so afraid to make a decision that she just endures all the beatings without a murmur. She is afraid to fight back, because she will be responsible for it and not just with words, but will suffer physically.

Women end up in intensive care. And this is not unusual. Women are beaten half to death, and sometimes to death. She is so afraid that she lets beat her. In those moments when she is beaten, she is silent. That's what fear means. Afraid at the cost of her own life.

She will be lucky to have a son. He would be her protector. It will not be lucky if a daughter is born who will also be beaten by her own father. The girl will develop a familiar pattern of behavior in family life and here is another victim has grown up. The daughter of a beaten woman will find for herself the same dad who will beat.

According to police reports, more than 60 % of women suffer domestic violence, but all remain silent. Few women have the strength to fight this attitude. We can't wait for help, as long as our society believes that the woman is responsible for the beatings. Nobody wants to get into someone else's family: "Let them figure it out." And a man, believe me, will figure it out with his wife. She will figure out that next time she will think several times before asking for help. She will think, because after - the punishment is not waiting for the man, but for her.

It's interesting. The woman needed help, but didn't get it. The man needed to be punished, but he didn't get it. Everything changed in a strange way. The man received help-no punishment, and the woman received punishment. No one was going to help her. Apparently, she doesn't have the right to help. She doesn't pay taxes for her safety. A man will be helped almost always.

With a few exceptions, the man will be punished. If he kills, he will be punished. This leads to a logical conclusion: that is, only a dead woman can get help. Posthumously.

19. Moms

A special category is women who have given birth and raised sons. I am by no means generalizing. There are not many such women, but they exist. This is a special kind of women. They were constantly searching for the perfect man, but alas – they never found. They were always dissatisfied with their husband, because he always fell short of the ideal.

It was these women who gave birth and raised not just sons, but real men, in their understanding. Each such mother brought up a man whom she would like to see next to her. Ideal man.

The time comes, and the son meets the girl he wants to marry. And then the advice starts, like: "why do you need it?", "you will meet a hundred of them", or my favorite: "you will have many more such prostitutes." How does she know that this is a young girl - a prostitute? Unclear. Maybe the two of them were standing on the highway, if such a certainty.

Now it is fashionable to give advice to your son in relation to girls. For example, mothers are advised to find a richer one. Quote: "always with an apartment and a good job. She may be older, or even much older. You can. The most important thing is that you are handsome and you need to be able to use it." Moms set their sons up for prostitution, for selling themselves. They themselves raise men who treat women as consumers.

Too many men do not know how to do anything at home. They do not know the basic things that a real man does without difficulty. They do not know how to serve themselves in everyday life. All these skills: Ironing a shirt, cooking dinner-all this comes from the family. This is what mother teaches as a teenager. But some mothers believe that all household duties should be carried by the wife of their beloved son. The woman thus discriminates against other women. She regards them as serving staff for her child. Women do it themselves. They themselves raise men with the wrong behavior model. Men who perceive women differently, but not as women. He can perceive a woman as a housewife or as an object of material goods. Moms do not teach their sons to love and respect, but only to use. This is pure discrimination against other women. This is sexism not on the part of men, but on the part of women.

In all seriousness, a man often believes that he is the most brutal and handsome, because his mother told him that. He cannot critically assess the situation, especially in choosing a wife for himself. Everything ends with such men more deplorably, as we think. Unfortunately, they never find anyone. There is no rich and old woman, no servant in the house. There is absolutely no one.

The modern woman has become different. A modern woman has the opportunity to develop, and therefore is confident in herself. She is no longer attracted to the "brutal son" with her mother, who constantly creeps into the family life of the newlyweds. The modern woman decides for herself who she wants to connect her fate with. And it may well be that she does not want to associate anything with anyone at all, but to devote herself to work. And this is normal. A woman has long realized that she can live as she not only deserves, but also wants.

Conclusion

There will be no equality until the rights of women and men are respected equally. There will be no equality until there is protection for victims of domestic violence, which means that women's support centers have been established.

There will be no equality until women themselves begin to defend their rights. Until women stop humiliating themselves as much as men.

I recently participated in an interesting dialogue. A woman compared herself to a monkey. She compared herself because she hadn't visited a beauty salon in a month. When I asked her: "why does she compare herself to a monkey?" She told me it was a joke.

As long as women make such humiliating jokes about themselves, there will be no equality. This will never happen. Women themselves do not allow equality.

There will be no equality until we women protect ourselves. We need solidarity to protect our rights and respect for each other.

I'm for real feminism. Not for the one where others compare feminists to the LGBT movement. Do not confuse feminism and homosexuality. These are different concepts. Feminism is about equal rights, not men's rights. Women should have their own rights, not someone else's.

I am for a feminism where men are not afraid of women. I am for a feminism where women are respected by men and their rights are respected, because women respect themselves.

But there is one important "but"! As long as there is no female President in the country, there is no feminism.

www.ingramcontent.com/pod-product-compliance
Lightning Source LLC
Chambersburg PA
CBHW062234150726
47991CB00006B/2568